BOW STREET R

BOW STREET RUNNER

By Charles Buchanan

Illustrated by Nick Horgan

ANGLIA *young* BOOKS

First published in 1992
by Anglia Young Books
Durhams Farmhouse
Ickleton
Saffron Walden, Essex CB10 1SR

Illustrations by Nick Horgan

British Library Cataloguing-in-Publication Data

A catalogue record for this book is available from the British Library

ISBN 1 871173 19 1

Typeset in Palatino
and printed in Great Britain by
Redwood Press Limited, Melksham, Wiltshire

AUTHOR'S NOTE

All the cases in this book are genuine ones and are documented by Henry Goddard himself in his autobiography. Although he called it, 'Memoirs of a Bow Street Runner', many of his earlier cases took place whilst he was a Runner at Great Marlborough Street. For the sake of continuity in such a small book the author has placed all the events in the story at Bow Street.

CHAPTER ONE

'Has the jury reached its verdict?'

'Yes, My Lord. We find the prisoner guilty as charged.'

The judge stood up, reached for his black cap and placed it on top of his tightly curled wig. There was a hush in the crowded courtroom.

'Robert Webster, you have been found guilty of stealing silver worth over 40 shillings from a dwelling house, which is a capital offence. Have you anything to say before I pass the sentence of death upon you?'

The prisoner clung onto the wooden rail of the dock. He looked at a man standing at the back of the courtroom. The man was called Henry Goddard, a 'Runner' from the famous Bow Street Police Station. It was Henry who had made the arrest.

Robert Webster turned to the judge and pleaded for his life.

'Mercy, mercy, My Lord!'

'Mercy to you Webster, would be a cruelty to others.'

Reverend Price, who had prosecuted the case, appealed to the judge. 'My Lord, in view of the prisoner's previous good character and the terrible affect such a sentence will have on his family, would it not be possible to show clemency?'

The judge was unmoved. He said, 'You have done your

duty Sir and I must, and shall, do mine.' He turned to the still weeping prisoner. 'Robert Webster, you will be taken from this court to a place of execution and there you shall be publicly hanged by the neck until you are dead. And may God have mercy upon your soul.'

Robert Webster let out a fearful cry and slumped to the floor. Pandemonium broke out in the courtroom, which was packed with people of all classes, including many society ladies, some of whom passed their scent bottles along to the Surgeon in order to revive the fainted prisoner, with whom they had great sympathy. He was young and so very handsome.

The condemned prisoner was led away, still in tears. Henry watched him go.

He should have been feeling pleased with himself. After all, it was his shrewd detective work which had caught Robert Webster. Whilst on foot patrol he had seen the young thief acting suspiciously outside a London jeweller's shop and soon afterwards arrested him for theft. But Henry felt a deep sense of unhappiness, even a little guilt, for his actions had sent the young man to the gallows. And for what? For stealing silver worth a little over 40 shillings. He believed the man should be punished; yes, most certainly. Transported to Australia maybe, but to face public execution in front of a blood thirsty mob? No, that wasn't justice; to him that was murder.

As he left the courtroom the grisly sentence was still being talked and argued about. Outside, men and women, both rich and poor, were making arrangements to attend the public hanging in a few days' time.

He overheard one finely dressed lady talking to her husband.

'I must write to my sister, Agnes. I'm certain she'll want

to bring her children to the hanging. We'll have the servants make up a picnic; but we'll have to set off early if we are to get a good view.'

Henry felt sick. Was it for this that he had become a 'Runner'? He decided to walk back to Bow Street, rather than take a Hackney cab. He needed the air.

Henry had joined the Runners through a sense of public duty, for London was known as the most lawless city in the world. He had started his police duties at Bow Street a few years earlier, where he was a member of the foot patrol. Then, he wore a uniform of blue coat and trousers, red waistcoat and black hat. It was carefully designed so as not to look like a soldier's uniform, for the English man in the street hated the thought of his personal freedom being threatened. He then moved to Great Marlborough Street station to become a fully fledged detective or 'Runner', but returned to Bow Street at the request of the station's chief magistrate, Sir Frederick Roe. Now he wore no uniform, but as a symbol of his authority, he carried a short staff with a crown on top. It was easy to hide in his coat, but he could produce it quickly when he had to.

Henry enjoyed his work very much. Every day was different and, at times, it was very exciting. It also allowed him to use his brain. He already had quite a reputation for solving cases through his powers of logical thought. Where other Runners often acted rashly, without thought, he would stop and think matters through carefully and once a decision had been reached, he acted swiftly and nothing could stop him from pursuing his man. Henry soon came to realise that not only policing methods needed to improve. The law itself had to be updated. It concerned him that a person could be hung for very minor offences, such as cutting down trees or stealing a sheep. Often, magistrates and juries saw the stupidity of some laws and refused to find a prisoner guilty, even if he had confessed to the crime, because it would end with the death penalty. But occasionally, there would still be a magistrate who stuck to the letter of the law, no matter how absurd the sentence was. Unfortunately, Robert Webster's judge was such a man.

• • • • •

A week after the trial, Henry was ordered by Sam Plank, his Chief Officer, to attend Robert Webster's execution at Tyburn.

'Couldn't you send someone else, Sir?' said Henry.

'As arresting officer, Goddard, it is your duty to attend,' said Sam Plank. 'Besides, the place will be swarming with pickpockets, so you'll have to be on your toes.'

The streets between the prison and the place of execution were lined with people. When Robert Webster was led past in a cart, they began jeering and pelting him with rotten vegetables. With Webster was the prison chaplain and a plain wooden coffin which would be his last resting place.

It was Henry's job to follow behind as a representative of the law. It was a very unpleasant experience.

At Tyburn, along with the scaffold, a stand had been erected which seated hundreds of people. From here the rich and the middle classes paid to watch the final agonies of the condemned. Today the crowds had started to arrive two hours before the execution was due to take place. Market traders set up their stalls to sell refreshments. Children were placed on their father's shoulders so that they could get a clear view. There was a carnival atmosphere.

4

Henry watched Robert Webster climb the scaffold and address the crowd. They instantly fell silent.

'I do confess my guilt and ask my master, who has always treated me with kindness, for his forgiveness. I regret the shame I have brought upon my family and I hope my example will serve as a warning to others.'

He sank to his knees and prayed. Then his hands were tied behind his back and a black bag placed over his head. The executioner asked him to stand and the rope was put around his neck. Henry looked up at the man on the scaffold and his heart was full of pity. He saw the executioner reach for the lever which would open the trap door and end Robert Webster's sad life. He turned away, unable to watch. A few seconds later he heard over a thousand people shout, 'Hurrah!'

Later that day Henry was called to the shop of a Mr Simpson, in Regent Street. When he arrived, he saw a man holding a young lady by the arm. She was dressed in a long silk gown and wore a hat with a lace veil that covered her face. In her hands she held a reticule.

'I caught her stealing ribbands from my shop and I want her charged,' said Mr Simpson.

'I'm sorry, Miss,' said Henry, 'but you must come with me to the police station.'

Outside, the lady's carriage, attended by two liveried servants, was waiting. The door opened and an elderly lady stepped out.

'I'm the girl's mother, officer. Is this really necessary? It's just an unfortunate mix up. I am willing to pay the shop keeper for the ribbands.'

'I'm afraid Mr Simpson wants the young lady officially charged, Madame.'

'This is intolerable, Sir! Wait until my husband hears of it!'. The elderly lady got back into the carriage and slammed the door shut. It then drove off at great speed.

'Come on, Miss,' said Henry, 'it's not far to walk.'

The young lady cried and sobbed all the way back to Bow Street police station. Henry allowed her to sit by the coal fire in the clerk's office whilst they waited for the magistrate to arrive.

Shortly afterwards there was a great commotion. A handsome, elderly gentleman burst into the room.

'I am a peer and a magistrate and not for £20,000 will I allow this case to be heard! Where can I find the sitting magistrate?'

'Next door, My Lord,' said Henry.

'Then no time must be lost. Show me the way!'

When the old gentleman returned, he took hold of the young lady's arm. Turning to Henry, he said, 'Good day to you, Sir!' They immediately left the building.

The magistrate arrived. 'This matter is a private one, Goddard. The young lady's mother is a countess and if the incident should come to light, it would ruin her daughter's marriage prospects. You will say no more about it. You do understand the delicacy of this matter, don't you?'

'Oh, yes, of course Sir,' said Henry, as he watched the magistrate leave the room. 'I just wonder if Robert Webster's mother does?'

CHAPTER TWO

'Mr Plank, Sir?'

'Yes, Goddard, what is it?'

'Mr Roe, the magistrate, and the Duke of Wellington would like to speak to you. They're both next door, in Mr Roe's office.'

Sam Plank, lifted his head from the report he was writing and stared hard at the smiling young man standing in front of him.

'Is this some kind of joke, Goddard?'

'No, Sir. The Iron Duke himself really is next door.'

After a moment's pause, Sam Plank stood up, took his black tail coat from the back of his chair and began to make his way towards the door. As he struggled to get the coat on, he turned,

'If this is another one of your practical jokes, Goddard, you'll be back on the night patrol.'

Henry could sense his boss's sudden discomfort at being summoned to see the Duke of Wellington, the hero of the battle of Waterloo and the conqueror of the French Emperor, Napoleon Bonaparte.

'Don't worry, Sir,' he said cheekily, 'I'm sure it's nothing to worry about. Maybe, the Iron Duke wants a personal body guard.'

Sam Plank almost choked. 'Get out of here, Goddard!'

Then as an afterthought, 'but don't leave the building. I may need you after the Duke has left.'

Henry liked Sam Plank. To many Runners, the Chief Officer seemed harsh and humourless, but he knew there was a softer, more caring side to his nature. It was Sam Plank who had helped Henry come to terms with the execution of Robert Webster.

'You're right, Webster didn't deserve to die for his crime,' Sam Plank had told him, 'but you were not responsible for his death. You were only doing your duty. It's your job to catch criminals and you do it very well, lad. Leave it to the politicians to sort out the law.'

'But the law can be so unfair,' argued Henry. 'Much of it needs to be changed. What's the point of having a modern professional approach to policing when the rest of the system is so out of date?'

'Times are changing and the law is struggling to keep up. That's why it is even more important that we do our job properly. If we don't, then certain people will try and get rid of us.'

'Is that possible?'

'I've heard talk of it. It seems almost certain that the Duke of Wellington will become Prime Minister and his views on law and order in this country are well known. It is rumoured that Sir Robert Peel will be put in charge of a new police force.'

'The ordinary man in the street won't like that,' said Henry.

'He won't have any choice in the matter. Remember, most ordinary men can't vote.'

After his meeting Sam Plank called Henry and another Runner, Tom Clements, into his office.

'Get yourselves down to the Traveller's Club at Pall Mall. There's been a break in. Some silver candlesticks have been stolen. See what you can find out. If you can catch the culprits, I have it on highest authority that the Duke of Wellington will be very grateful.' He looked at Henry. 'So it's important we don't disappoint him. And another thing,' added the Chief Officer, as the two men turned to go,'keep your enquiries discreet and don't talk to any newspaper reporters!'

Henry and Tom Clements took a hackney cab to the Traveller's Club, a drive of about fifteen minutes through the busy London traffic. They were immediately shown the closet from which the silver candlesticks had been taken.

'I came to the closet at about 8 o'clock this morning,' said the butler. 'To my astonishment, I found that the locks had been forced and that seven silver candlesticks were missing. I'd put them there myself at 11 o'clock last night, just before I went to bed.'

The two Runners made an inspection of the club in an attempt to find out exactly where the burglars had got in. They checked all the doors and windows, along with the roof, skylights and gutters. Nothing had been forced.

'What do you reckon then?' asked Tom Clements.

'They must have come in from the street, through the front hall, and then made off the same way,' said Henry. 'It's the only possible explanation.'

'Let's talk to the hall porter,' said Tom. 'Maybe he can remember seeing someone come in.'

'No, Sir,' said the hall porter, 'I'll swear that no one came in through the front door who shouldn't have. I bolted it at half past ten last night, and put the key into my pocket.'

Henry called over the Club Secretary. 'There can only be one conclusion to our enquiries. If the butler and the hall porter are telling the truth, then the stolen candlesticks must still be in the building somewhere. With your permission, Sir, we will send back to Great Marlborough Station for some assistance to search the premises.'

'Of course, Gentleman,' said the Secretary. 'As you wish.'

Whilst the two Runners were waiting for their colleague to arrive, they decided to question the butler and the hall porter again. They started with the butler.

'Think,' said Henry. 'Are you sure that no unauthorized person entered through the front door last night?'

'Certain,' said the butler. 'Except of course for the sweeps.'

'What!' yelled Henry. 'Why didn't you tell us this before? When did they come?'

'At about five o'clock.'

'Did you let them in?'

'But of course. They said they had been sent by Cook's in Argyll Street.'

'How do you know they were from Cooks's?'

'Because they told me they were.'

'After they had done the sweeping,' said Henry, suspicious of the butler's apparent forgetfulness, 'how much soot did they take out?'

'About half a sack full.'

'Not very much for a building this size, is it?'

'No, I suppose it's not. I didn't really give it much thought at the time.'

The reinforcement Runner, by the name of George Schofield, had now arrived.

'Begin searching for the missing candlesticks,' said Henry. 'Tom and I will pay a visit to Mr Cook of Argyll Street. And keep an eye on the butler and hall porter. It's possible they are in on this.'

At Argyll Street Mr Cook was not amused.

'I certainly did not send any of my sweeps to the Traveller's Club and I take great offence, Sir, at my name being dragged into this sordid affair.'

'I'm sure the Duke of Wellington will appreciate your co-operation, Mr Cook,' said Henry.

'The Duke of Wellington? Oh, well of course,' said Mr Cook, his tone of voice changing immediately. 'I will do what ever I can to help. Please tell the Duke that.'

Henry smiled. 'I'll do that Mr Cook.'

· · · · ·

Later in the afternoon Henry and Tom Clements reported back to Sam Plank.

'Well,' said Sam, 'what do you make of it?'

'I think there are two possibilities,' said Henry. 'Either the hall porter and the butler are the culprits, or it was done by the bogus sweeps.'

'What about this Mr Cook in Argyll Street? Is he honest do you think?'

'I believe so,' said Henry. 'But it might be as well to have him followed, just in case.'

'Right,' said Sam. 'I'll also have the hall porter and butler followed. What are you two going to do?'

'Tom and I thought we'd go round the pubs tonight and see what information we can pick up,' said Henry. 'If the thieves are local, then someone will know something.'

• • • • •

They began their investigations in the St Giles and Seven Dials districts of the city. Here life was hard, especially for the childen. People lived in poverty and squalor and many turned to petty crime, such as pickpocketing, to survive, even though the punishment for being caught could be savage. To escape the harshness of life many of the poor working classes spent much of their free time in the public houses or inns. Here, for a few hours at least, they could forget their misery.

To Henry and his fellow Runners, the public houses were a very important source of information. Often criminals who had committed a crime would boast when they were drunk, and there was always someone who would turn them in for a reward. All Henry and Tom had to do was spread the word and wait.

That night they were in luck. A woman, who was

obviously the worse for drink, approached them whilst they were sitting at a table in a public house called 'The White Lion'.

''Ere, I got some information for you.' She could hardly stand. 'About that robbery at their Lordships' club in Pall Mall. But yer'll have to make it worth my while. If ever he finds out I shopped 'im, my life won't be woth a farthing.' She looked around the room to see if she was being watched. Then she whispered a name. 'Sam White. He's one of them. He's living with a so-called friend of mine, Nance Castle, in Bethnal Green. He sold two of them candlesticks to old Solomon, the pawnbroker. His shop is at the end of the street here.'

Next morning Henry and Tom went to old Solomon's shop. They pretended to be antique collectors and sure enough the two stolen candlesticks were offered to them. They arrested Solomon and took him to Bow Street. Sam Plank then ordered the arrest of Sam White.

'Right, Goddard, take Clements, Schofield and Avis with you. Avis can identify this Sam White. He says he's a nasty piece of work, so you'd better go along armed.

The streets around Bethnal Green were full of people. A protest march by the Weaver's Guild was taking place. Hundreds of people marching to a brass band waving banners with slogans such as 'Starvation', 'The Workhouse', 'We Are In Want Of Bread', written on them. Hundreds more were watching and cheering from the pavements. All were chanting: the noise was deafening.

'I can see him!' shouted Avis. 'Over there. That man talking to the dark haired woman. That's Sam White!'

Henry looked at a man dressed in a short, well worn jacket. He was stockily built with a great bull neck.

'Right, let's grab him!'

The four Runners dashed across the road through the marching procession. Sam White instinctively looked around and saw four men making towards him. He ran into the middle of the protest marchers. 'Murder! Murder!' he called out. 'They're going to kill me!'

There was uproar. Henry, being the fastest Runner, got to Sam White first. He grabbed him by the collar with one hand and with the other took hold of his wrist. Sam White struggled violently and tried to throw Henry over his shoulder. The other three Runners arrived. Avis and Schofield went to Henry's aid whilst Clements tried to keep the angry crowd at bay with his cutlass. In the scuffle, Henry was thrown to the ground, but he still managed to keep hold of Sam White and pull him down on top of him. Unfortunately, Avis and Schofield also fell and Henry had to bear the weight of all three. But even though in great pain, he did not relinquish his hold on his man.

By now the crowd, who thought that Sam White was a weaver like themselves, were shouting, 'Rescue! Rescue!' and Nance Castle was crying. 'They're taking my Sam! Don't let them!'

The situation looked bad for Henry and his colleagues. The weavers, who had made a circle around them, began to close in.

The Runners were saved from serious injury by the arrival of a dozen officers from the local station. One of the crowd had run and informed them that there was trouble in the street.

Henry finally managed to get Sam White into a Hackney cab which took him speedily to Bow Street, where Sam Plank took the prisoner into custody.

• • • • •

'Well, Gentlemen,' said the Duke of Wellington, finishing his glass of port. 'I must congratulate you on your speedy and successful conclusion to this matter. Rest assured, I shall inform the House.'

'When old man Solomon saw that Sam White had been arrested,' said Henry, 'he decided to save his own neck and turn King's evidence. Spilling the beans on Sam White will get him a lessser sentence. Fortunately, we were able to recover all the stolen candlesticks. Sam White also gave us the names of his two accomplices.'

Sam Plank addressed the Duke. 'I must say, Sir, it was very decent of you and the club to request that Sam White's death sentence be commuted to transportation for life.'

'I have seen too many lives wasted unnecessarily,' said the Duke. 'If people are to respect the law, then sentences must reflect the nature and seriousness of the crime. After all, man, it is almost the 1830's. That's why if my friends and I get our way in the House, the whole question of policing and the role of the magistrates will be reviewed.'

'Will that mean the end of the Runners, Sir?' asked Henry.

Sam Plank's face turned bright red at the impudence of such a question to the future Prime Minister of the country.

The Iron Duke smiled. 'So you've heard the rumours,

then? No, of course not, Goddard. How could we disband an organisation which employs the like of men such as yourself? Rest assured, if I have anything to do with it, the Runners will continue to function alongside any new police force that comes into operation. And now, Gentlemen, is there any favour I can grant to show my appreciation of a job well done?'

For a moment there was silence. Then Henry said. 'Yes, Sir. There is one thing you can grant me. I would like a week's leave.'

'What!' exclaimed Sam Plank, unable to control himself. 'A week's leave? What on earth could justify a week's leave?'

Henry smiled broadly. 'I'm getting married.'

CHAPTER THREE

'You're a very lucky man, Goddard, that's all I can say,' said Sam Plank, draining his glass of champagne.

'Why thank you Mr Plank, Sir,' said Henry. 'I hope you are enjoying the reception.'

'Capital, old lad, capital,' Sam Plank winked. 'Especially the champagne.'

'Nothing but the best today, Sir. This is the happiest day of my life.'

'She certainly is a beautiful young woman,' said Sam. 'Where did you meet her?'

'When I first joined Bow Street as a foot patrol man. I was on duty at the Drury Lane theatre one night, when she ran into the foyer. I was wearing my footman's uniform and she asked me to go with her to Covent Garden, as a Gentleman by the name of Mr Spring had been robbed of his gold watch in the street. That was five years ago.'

'The detective in Sam Plank was curious. 'Did you catch the thief?'

'No, but I got the watch back. I must admit I think it was that which impressed Rose more than my good looks.'

'Modesty,' said Sam Plank, 'has never been one of your greatest virtues, has it Goddard?'

Henry laughed. 'No, Sir, I'm, afraid it hasn't.'

Sam Plank drank another glass of champagne. 'Well?' he said, still curious.

'Sir?' said Henry, feigning ignorance.

'How did you get the watch back?'

'Oh, I found it under some cabbage leaves in Covent Garden.'

'So it was luck then?'

'Certainly not, Sir,' said Henry, pretending to be offended.

'But you couldn't have known it was there,' said Sam.

'I didn't know which particular leaf, but I did know I would find it in that area.'

'How?'

'Pure logic. Mr Spring had called out to the thieves to stop. I reasoned, therefore, that there was a strong possibility that the thieves might have panicked and dropped the watch, rather than risk being caught with it in their possession. And I was right. More champagne, Mr Plank, Sir?'

The wedding reception was being held at Henry and Rose's new home at 12 Robert Street, near Hampstead Heath. Most of Henry's guests came from Bow Street. Along with Sam Plank, there was Tom Clements and George Schofield. They spent much of the afternoon debating police issues, much to the annoyance of the ladies.

'I think it's the thin edge of the wedge,' said George Schofield. 'We all know that Sir Robert Peel wants his New Police to be the only police authority in the city of London.'

'In the whole country, if he gets his way,' said Tom Clements.

'But the New Police haven't got a detective branch,' argued Henry. 'They're just a preventative force, there to take over from the old "Charlies".'

'Yes, but for how long?' said Sam Plank.

'I've heard the poor devils are only being paid 19 shillings a week (95p),' said Tom Clements.

'What!' exclaimed Schofield. 'How can a family man survive on 19 shillings a week?'

'According to Sir Robert Peel, very comfortably,' said Sam Plank.

Schofield blew out his cheeks and waved a hand. 'Oh, well, a rich man like Sir Robert Peel must know what he's talking about, mustn't he?'

'Now, now, Schofield,' said Sam Plank. 'Remember your station.'

Schofield immediately stood to attention and saluted. 'Yes, Sir! One must remember to keep in one's place and not question the actions of one's betters. Sorry, Sir!' He spun round and walked away.

'He's had too much to drink, that's all,' said Henry. 'He's a fine officer.'

'That's as maybe,' said Sam Plank. 'But the discipline of the Runners is what makes us different from the New Police and indispensable to the Government.'

The rather heated discussion was interrupted by Henry's new bride.

'Gentlemen. The ladies at this reception are calling this police briefing to a close. You will return to your wives and that includes you, Henry Goddard.' She smiled at the group of startled men. 'And that's an order.'

'I'll tell you what, Goddard,' said Sam Plank, watching Rose mingle with the other guests, 'if ever women get to join the force, then the new Mrs Goddard would get my vote as Chief of Police.'

'Don't be ridiculous, Mr Plank, Sir,' said Henry. 'Who can ever imagine the day when women will be allowed to join the police?'

'Yes,' said Tom Clements. 'You might as well say that women would one day be able to vote at a General Election! Or that a woman could become Prime Minister!'

They all laughed.

· · · · ·

The 'rat-a-tat' of the brass door handle echoed up and down the deserted street. Eventually, it had the desired effect.

'Rose, Rose, I've got to get up. There's someone knocking at the door.'

'Mmmh? But it's our wedding night. No one can expect you to get up and work on your wedding night.' She fumbled for her husband's pocket watch which lay on the bedside table.' It's two o'clock in the morning!'

'But it might be important, dear. I've got to get up and see.'

Henry jumped out of bed, put on his dressing gown over

his nightshirt, and went downstairs. He opened the door and found Tom Clements standing on the step.

'The Chief wants you to come with me right away. We're to meet him at Tyburn Gate. He's received information that there is going to be a duel between two Gentlemen at Wormwood Scrubbs.'

'I'll get dressed and be back down in five minutes.'

Upstairs, Rose Goddard lit a candle. 'I suppose I'd better get used to this kind of thing,' she said, as Henry returned. 'But on our wedding night!'

Henry and Tom Clements made their way along the deserted streets. They were in complete darkness until they reached the gas lit area of the city centre. Occasionally, they would see a Bow Street night patrol officer walking the streets, no doubt dreaming, as Henry had once done, of becoming a 'Runner'.

Sam Plank was waiting at Tyburn gate when Henry and Tom Clements arrived. The chief officer had already hired a post-chaise to take them speedily to their destination.

'Sorry about this Goddard,' said Sam Plank, as they drove off, 'but you and Clements are the officers needed for this job. I hope Mrs Goddard is not too distressed.'

'Don't worry, Sir, I'm sure Rose will forgive you, this once.'

Looking extremely uncomfortable, Sam Plank ran a forefinger along the inside of his collar.

They soon arrived at the lane which led to Wormwood Scrubbs, an open heathland from which, in the distance, one could see the silhouetted outline of the grand city of London.

The post-chaise was sent away, and they swiftly hid themselves behind a very high hedge. All was quiet and still, except for the early stirrings of skylarks, who sang to herald the dawn.

'They say the Duke of Wellington once fought a duel,' said Tom Clements, blowing into his hands to keep out the early morning chill.

'So did Sir Robert Peel,' said Sam Plank.

'But Sir Robert has spoken out against dualling,' said Henry.

'Well, as the man in charge of the New Police, he has to,' said Tom. 'I mean, he can hardly talk of breaking the law himself, can he?'

'But he did break the law,' said Henry.

'Not exactly,' said Tom. 'The duel never actually happened and the incident did take place over fifteen years ago, when the law turned a blind eye to duelling.'

'Why didn't the duel take place?' asked Henry.

'Because the "gentleman" that Sir Robert was to fight was arrested. Now what did the newspapers write? Ah, yes, that's it. "Sir Robert sought the reputation for valour without incurring any risk".'

'You mean, they called him a coward?' said Henry horrified. 'But that's libellous. Did Sir Robert sue?'

'Not that I can recall,' said Tom. 'Do you know if he did, Mr Plank?'

The Chief of Police looked uncomfortable. He did not like his men questioning the actions of their superiors. 'I can't remember,' he said stiffly.

'What do you think of duelling as a way of settling arguments, Mr Plank, Sir?' said Henry.

'It is now against the law and that's good enough for me. If we catch gentlemen duelling, we will arrest them. That's all there is to it.'

'Even if one of these "gentlemen" happens to be the Prime Minister of Great Britain?' said Henry.

'Even if he was the King of the British Empire, Goddard. Now both of you, stop gibbering and concentrate on your job!'

Henry smiled. His Chief of Police was a real professional.

'Listen!' Tom Clements whispered. 'I think I can hear the sound of carriage wheels.'

'Quick, Goddard. Shin up this tree and get a better look,' Sam Plank ordered.

Henry soon found himself amongst the boughs and green foliage of a tall elm tree. On the horizon he could make out three carriages approaching. They stopped about twenty yards in front of the young Runner. Henry counted eight men. He slid down the elm tree and reported his observations to Sam Plank.

'Right, lads. We must time this just right. Go too early and we won't have enough grounds to arrest them. Go too late and we could have a dead body on our hands.'

Two men got out of the first coach and made their way to

one side of the clearing. Another two stepped down from the second and went to the opposite side. Lastly, one man stepped out of the remaining coach carrying a black case and took up a position between the other two parties. He opened the case and held it chest high in front of him. Then two of the men, one from either side of the clearing, took off their coats and top hats and gave them to the men standing next to them.

Henry watched in growing anticipation. The inside of his stomach began to churn as he waited for Sam Plank to give the word. He saw the two coatless men walk slowly towards each other. When they reached the middle, they both took a long barreled pistol from out of the black case and lined up against each other, back to back. So far, not a word had been spoken by any of the participants.

Faintly, Henry heard the third man speak.

'Gentlemen, on the count of one, you will both begin to walk. When I reach the count of ten, you will stop and turn around. You may then take aim and fire your weapons. Are you both ready?'

The two men nodded.

'One . . .'

'Now!' said Sam Plank.

Henry dashed out from behind the hedge and ran as fast as he could. All the while he shouted.

'Stop! Stop!'

By the count of 'eight' Henry reached the man with the suitcase. He was quickly joined by Tom Clements and a very wheezy Sam Plank. The two duellists looked on in astonishment.

'My name is Sam Plank, Chief Police Officer of Bow Street and you gentlemen are under arrest for a breach of the peace. Please hand over your weapons to my officers.'

The men put up no resistance. They were escorted back to Bow Street and charged.

• • • • •

It was a weary-eyed Runner who returned home to his new wife in Robert Street at six o'clock that morning. Rose was waiting for him with a cup of tea. She wanted to hear all about it.

Henry only reached as far as his shinny up the elm tree, when he began to nod off.

'Bed!' ordered Rose. 'And if we get another knock at the door, I'll tell them you're indisposed.'

'Mr Plank won't like that, my love,' said a yawning Henry.

'Then Mr Plank will have to come and get you himself,' said Rose.

Henry smiled as he got up. 'Then I'm bound to have a good sleep.' He made for the door.

'What do you mean?' asked Rose.

'He's scared of you.'

Climbing the stairs Henry laughed to himself as he thought of his Rose and Sam Plank.

'Maybe, one day women will get the vote!'

CHAPTER FOUR

'Have you heard the news?' said Sam Plank, addressing his officers in a sombre mood. 'The King passed away this morning.'

'Good riddance, that's all I can say,' said George Schofield. He looked at the solemn faces of the men around him, amongst them Henry Goddard. 'Well, I mean, as a Monarch he was an absolute disgrace, wasn't he?'

'He was still your King, George,' said Henry.

'The Coronation of the late King's brother will take place in Westminster Abbey later in the Summer,' Sam Plank informed them.

George Schofield could not hide his derision. 'What? "Sailor Billy"? A sixty-five year old drunkard?'

'King William IV to you, Schofield!' snapped Sam Plank. 'If you are not careful, that loose tongue of yours will land you in trouble.'

'It's a free country, Mr Plank. I can say anything I please. There's no law against that . . . yet. I say we ought to get rid of the monarchy and become a republic.'

'The monarchy represents stability and continuity, George,' said Henry. 'If we get rid of it, it could lead to civil war. It did so in France.'

'Maybe, but it didn't in America. The royal family of this country are ridiculed by every social class. You mark my words, they won't last much longer.'

'If you insist on talking revolution, Schofield,' said Sam Plank, 'then do so in your own time, which this isn't. Now out you go and do something really useful, like catching criminals! And that goes for the rest of you!'

Most of the Runners immediately left the office to take up their duties in the city. Henry sat at his desk in order to write up his report concerning the conclusion of a successful case.

Madame Vestry, a famous actress who performed regularly at the Drury Lane theatre, had had some money stolen from her carriage whilst she was rehearsing. Henry was convinced the culprit was the actress's page, George Walker, who had mysteriously disappeared after the theft. It seemed the young lad had talked about going to the West Country. Making further enquiries, Henry learned of a coach going to Oxford and Cheltenham, the following morning, from a local inn. Henry arrived early next morning and saw a youth pay for a breakfast of eggs, bread, butter and tea with a five pound note. When he left, Henry asked the landlord to show him the bank note. The number read 5743 and was one of the notes stolen from Madame Vestry. Henry immediately went outside and arrested Walker. A few days later he was sentenced to seven years transportation in Australia. This form of punishment was becoming increasingly popular. The convicted criminal, and often they could be children, was sent away to the other side of the world to serve his sentence working in prison camps. On being released, the prisoner had to pay his own fare back to England. Consequently, many never saw their families again.

As he read through his finished report, George Schofield came back into the office.

'Henry, there's a rough looking navvy outside. Says he must speak to you.'

Henry went outside accompanied by Schofield. He recognised the man waiting for him. He had approached Henry when he was arresting George Walker and asked if he was a police officer and that if he was, he had some important information to sell. Henry had given the man his card.

'So you've found me then?' said Henry.

The man laughed nervously. 'My name's Joe Bealey. I've never been to Lunnon before. You remember that burglary at Hawstead Hall in Lincolnshire about a year ago? Well I know where you can find the fourth member of the gang. And for the £100 reward I'm willing to take you to him.'

'Yes, I remember,' said Henry. 'The other three members of the gang were all caught and hanged at Lincoln Castle. But the fourth, Dick Poacher, is still at large.'

'And I know's where he is,' said Joe gleefully. 'He's working with a hundred other navvies, digging the Oxford canal.'

Henry immediately took Joe to the sitting magistrate and obtained a warrant for Dick Poacher's arrest. Then, with the approval of Sam Plank, Henry and Schofield arranged to meet Joe the next morning at the 'Swan-with-two-necks' inn, where they would catch the mail-coach.

'How long's it going to take to get there?' said Joe, as the mail-coach set off on the first leg of the journey. He had never ridden inside before. The fare was too costly for a working man like him. His only other experience of public transport was sitting on top of a conventional coach next to the driver.

'The mail-coach is the fastest vehicle on the roads and can

travel at about 12 miles an hour,' said Henry. 'So we should reach Northampton in about seven hours.'

'That's if we're not held up,' quipped Joe.

The mail-coach was always a potential target for daring highwaymen. Only wealthy people could travel in them and often there was rich picking to be had.

'We've got the guard travelling on top with his blunderbuss,' said Henry. 'He should act as a deterrent.'

'And we've got our own pistols,' said Tom Schofield, patting the inside of his jacket.

The mail-coach was pulled by a team of six horses which were changed every seven miles at the 'stages', or inns, along the main highways. The conditions of these important link roads had improved dramatically over the past thirty years, through the efforts of engineers like Thomas Telford and John Macadam, who, with their teams of labourers, were transforming the road network. It was said the new roads extended the working lives of the horses from three to seven years.

Being the middle of July, Henry found the journey very pleasant. It was a warm day but a cool refreshing breeze blew in through the open windows. In winter such travel could be very uncomfortable indeed.

'Do you think the steam locomomotive will ever seriously challenge the horse drawn carriage?' Henry asked George Schofield, as they rumbled along through open countryside.

'I doubt it. It's just a novelty, which I think will quickly lose public interest.'

'They do say, that at the Rainhill trials last year, George

Stephenson got his locomotive up to a speed of over thirty miles an hour.'

'I don't believe that,' said George Schofield. 'You know how the daily papers like to exaggerate things. It sells papers, doesn't it? Anyway, it's unnatural, unreliable and from all accounts extremely dangerous. Look what happened to William Huskisson, of the Board of Trade at the opening of this Liverpool and Manchester Railway. Killed he was. No, the railways will never catch on.'

Joe Bealey slept through most of the journey, no doubt because of his constant habit of nipping into the inns for a tot of rum every time the mail-coach stopped to change horses. After the fifth change Henry suggested to Joe that he forgo his 'tot', but Joe said that if they tried to stop him, he would get off the coach and go elsewhere.

'Fine,' said George Schofield, 'Go ahead. Mr Goddard and myself would get on much better without you.'

The reply tempered Joe's drinking. After all, he could buy as many tots of rum as he desired with the £100 reward money. For the rest of the journey he sat subdued.

They arrived at the Angel Inn, Northampton, at 4 o'clock in the afternoon. Joe said he was famished and so Henry paid for him to eat a meal of salt beef and carrots. The navvy also needed three pints of beer and another tot of rum to wash it down! They still had eight miles to go before they reached their final destination, a village named Weedon. As there was no coach going that way, Henry suggested that they set off to walk there that evening.

After covering four miles, with Joe grumbling all way, they stopped for a rest. Joe said he was sleepy and the two Runners allowed him to lie down under a nearby rick. He was soon fast asleep and snoring like a pig. An hour later, Henry tried to wake him but found it impossible to do so.

'What are we going to do now?' said Schofield. 'He's drunk so much, he might not wake up until morning.'

'We'll give him another half hour,' said Henry.

It was nine o'clock in the evening and the light was fading fast when they finally managed to rouse Joe from his slumbers. He immediately complained that he had a great thirst. Henry knocked on the door of a nearby cottage and asked an old man for some refreshment. From a nearby well, he produced a bucket of clear cool water and dipped a large jug into it. Joe downed this in two draughts and immediately appeared fresh and alert.

The old man wanted nothing for the water, but George Schofield slipped a sixpenny piece into his hands, and the travellers bid him goodnight.

There was no stopping Joe now. He strode off in front at a great pace and they covered the other four miles in less than an hour. They booked into a village inn and arranged for Joe to have some supper, which consisted of cold roast beef, half a loaf of bread, several big onions and a quart of beer. As Henry and George Schofield went to eat their light supper in the adjoining parlour room, a master sweep and his apprentice came into the tap room and on seeing Joe tucking away asked the landlord if they could have the same.

'The beef's all gone. The best I can do is bread and cheese.'

'That'll do fine' said the master sweep, 'And give us two quarts of beer to go with it.'

The sweeps sat down at Joe's table and soon got into conversation with him. After finishing the beer all three took to drinking tots of rum and hot water and smoking pipes. Joe then amused them by saying he could unscrew his nose and immediately proceeded to use his big brawny hands, along with the grating of his teeth, to give the desired effect.

The master sweep then challenged Joe to a 'friendly' wrestling match. Joe accepted. The tables and chairs were pushed to one side and the contest began.

After several minutes of rolling around the floor, it seemed that Joe was getting the better of the master sweep and so his apprentice jumped in to help. The 'friendly' contest turned into an ugly brawl. On hearing the noise the maid servant came into the room. She was terrified and cried out, 'Murder!'

The landlord ran into the parlour room and asked the two Runners, who had been oblivious to Joe's antics, for help. Henry and George Schofield rushed in. Henry immediately tried to part the warring factions. Both Joe and the master sweep were covered with facial blood. Schofield drew his pistol and threatened to shoot if the two parties did not stop. This so alarmed the landlord, that he thought Henry and Schofield must be robbers. He sent his maid servant to fetch the soldiery from the local barracks nearby.

Two minutes later, half a dozen soldiers, dressed in brightly coloured uniforms of red coats, white breeches and black boots marched in, all carrying loaded muskets. The lieutenant in charged fired his weapon through the ceiling, whilst his men seized hold of everyone, including Henry and George Schofield.

'Right, you lot! You are all under arrest!'

CHAPTER FIVE

It took Henry some minutes to convince the lieutenant that he and Schofield were really police officers on official duty and not armed robbers. Once satisfied, the lieutentant, after giving Joe Bealey and the two sweeps a stern lecture, withdrew his men. The sweeps left and Henry apologised to the inn keeper for the misunderstanding.

The two Runners managed to get Joe into bed. The navvy immediately fell into a deep sleep and was soon snoring loudly.

'I think we ought to take his hat, boots and trousers,' said Henry.'Just in case our troublesome friend wakes up in the night and decides to do a runner.'

Exhausted, Henry and his companion finally retired to their own beds in the early hours of the morning. As he drifted into unconsciousness, Henry felt a little tingle of anticipation in his stomach, at the thought of what the morning might bring.

• • • • •

Henry and George Schofield were up and about by seven o'clock. They went and roused Joe who was still snoring soundly. The rough navvy was unaware of the precautions Henry had taken and he was soon tucking into a breakfast of eggs, bacon and beer. At nine o'clock the three set off on the last stage of their journey by foot.

From the outset Joe was in a quarrelsome mood. He kept

demanding money for rum every time they passed a roadside inn and sulked if he was refused. Henry tried to humour him.

'I must say, Joe you have a remarkable set of teeth and they appear so white. What do you clean them with?'

Joe laughed. 'Why, with beer of course!'

Joe continued to chuckle to himself for another couple of miles, until they reached the town of Rugby, which was only three miles from their final destination, the Oxford canal at Newbold. Here Joe sat down and flatly refused to go any further. He demanded the reward money before he went and pointed out his pal, Dick Poacher. Henry tried to reason with him.

'Look, Joe. We can't give you the money first. It isn't the way the law works. You have to identify Dick Poacher, we arrest him and he stands trial. Then you get your money. I'm sorry, but that's the way it is.'

Joe did not reply but continued to sit mumbling under his breath.

'We're going to need some help in this matter,' Henry said to George Schofield.

'What do you suggest?' said George.

'I'll try and find the local constable and see if he can assist us. You stay here and keep an eye on Joe. He's beginning to get edgy.'

The office of constable was not a full time job like the Runners. Usually he was a small tradesman who undertook the duty in his spare time. After questioning various local people, Henry tracked the Rugby constable down to a small butcher's shop. He introduced himself and informed him of their business.

The constable was chopping up a sheep's carcass as he listened. He brought the small axe down with a thud.

'It's a very serious undertaking, Mr Goddard, Sir. These navvies are a rough lot and they stick together. I reckon you'll be needing the assistance of at least twenty armed soldiers.'

'I'm afraid there can be no soldiers,' said Henry. 'We must do this thing quickly and quietly. We can't afford to arouse their suspicions.'

The constable scratched his head. 'Well, there's the Tring brothers, our local blacksmiths. They are a formidable pair and for a small fee, I'm sure they will help.'

'Good,' said Henry. 'Let's get organised.'

· · · · ·

Henry was introduced to the Tring brothers who, for a fee of a guinea each, agreed to help. Henry took them to the local magistrate to get them sworn in as temporary constables. The brothers then organised transport to take them all the last three miles to where the navvies were digging the Oxford Canal. The two Runners and Joe were to travel by post-chaise and the constable and Tring brothers were to follow fifteen minutes later in a trap.

As they prepared to set off, Joe sat down again and refused to budge. It was obvious to Henry that the man was losing his nerve.

'I can't go through with it,' said Joe. 'If Dick finds out that I split on him, I'm a dead man. Just give me the reward now and let me go home.'

'It's too late to back out now, Joe,' said George Schofield. 'If you don't come with us, we'll go alone and find Dick. When we've arrested him, we'll tell all his mates that it was you who gave us the information.'

Joe was terrified. 'No! Don't do that! I'll come, I'll come.'

· · · · ·

They set Joe down about half a mile from where the navvies were working. The magistrate had informed them that when their shift finished at six o'clock, they would go into the nearby inn for food and refreshment. The plan was that Henry should go into the inn first, disguised as a pedlar and for Joe to come in a few minutes after him. George Schofield was to stay outside. The trap, carrying the magistrate and the Tring brothers, was to stop a little distance away and await the given signal.

Henry walked into the inn, dressed in a check shirt, billy-cock hat and a fustian jacket, and bid good evening to the innkeeper. He ordered a glass of beer along with bread and cheese and sat down at an empty table. Two minutes later, Joe Bealey came in, and as instructed made no acknowledgement of Henry. He ordered a glass of beer and sat down at a table at the other end of the room.

As the clock in the tap room struck six o'clock, the navvies began to flood into the inn. They all carried either picks or shovels, which they leant against the bar. They all called for glasses of beer and about thirty of them ordered food. Presently, a tall, powerfully built man entered, carrying a shovel on his shoulder. He walked straight over to the bar and ordered bacon and eggs. Whilst he waited, he played a popular music hall tune on the bar top with his knuckles.

When his supper was brought the man sat down at a

table and made short work of the meal. At this point, Joe Bealey came over to him with a full glass of beer, and as pre-arranged with Henry said.

'Come, Dick lad! Take a drink!' He then looked across at Henry in an exaggerated manner.

Dick took the glass and drained half of it in one draught. Joe then finished the other half off and called for another. After paying for it, he placed it on Dick's table, took hold of his hand and shook it. Then he said, much too dramatically, 'Well, goodnight, Dick,' and sauntered out of the inn, leaving Henry alone, smoking a pipe.

Outside, George Schofield sat perched on a stile reading a newspaper. Joe went over to him.

'I done it. I reckon Dick'll be out soon.'

'Here's two sovereigns,' said George Schofield. 'Get yourself back down to London and lay low for a few days. Then come and see us.'

Ten minutes later, George Schofield saw Dick Poacher leave the inn accompanied by a dozen or so fellow navvies. Walking out behind them was Henry. Whilst Dick and his mates made off in the direction of the waiting post-chaise, Henry was happy to follow along, but when they suddenly made a turn down a narrow lane, he acted swiftly.

With no regard for his own safety, he ran up to Dick and put his hand on his shoulder.

'Dick Poacher, I am a police officer up from London, and I have a warrant here for your arrest in connection with the robbery at Hawstead Hall, in Lincolnshire. Consider yourself in my custody.'

'If you don't let go of me,' hissed Dick, raising his shovel above his head, 'I'll brain you!'

Undeterred by Dick's threat, Henry seized hold of the wanted man's arm and pushed his shoulder under his armpit, causing Dick to drop the shovel.

The rest of Dick's mates had, at first, continued down the lane. Now that they realised something was up they turned round to help their struggling friend. Even the sight of a dozen rugged men coming towards him did not make Henry let go of Dick Poacher's arm. Writhing in agony, he shouted.

'They'll have you now, mate. They'll beat you to pulp!'

At this moment, George Schofield appeared brandishing a brace of pistols. He put one of them to Dick's head and called to the others:

'By God, if you don't back off, I'll blow his brains out!'

The navvies held off as Henry and George Schofield slowly backed their man up the lane towards the post-chaise. The gang of pickaxe and shovel wielding navvies kept up with them, waiting for their chance to strike. Suddenly, Dick was grabbed from behind. George Schofield spun round quickly and prepared to fire one of his pistols. He stopped himself just in the nick of time, for it was one of the Tring brothers that had seized hold of Dick. The other brother and the magistrate, also took hold of the still struggling prisoner.

'Am I glad to see you three,' said Henry.

Dick Poacher began to panic.

'Come on!' he shouted to the other navvies, now

numbering over thirty. 'Come on! Isn't there a man amongst you?'

Somehow, Dick pulled free of his captors, but fell to the ground. Henry immediately dived on top of him and they rolled over the flints and stones of the road. One of the Tring brothers managed to put a pair of handcuffs on Dick and, with Henry's assistance, pulled him back to his feet.

Seeing their friend almost struggle free, the gang of navvies made a sudden surge forward. It was a desperate situation. They were forced back again by George Schofield discharging one of his pistols above their heads.

Henry called over to a young boy passing on a pony and gave him half a crown to go down the road and tell the waiting post-chaise to hurry to their assistance. Meanwhile, Dick Poacher was slowly being dragged along, kicking and swearing.

Within minutes the post-chaise arrived and the magistrate and the Tring brothers tried to force Dick into it, whilst Henry drew his own pistol and went to support his companion against the angry mob. Dick knew that the game was nearly up and he desperately resisted. He bit and kicked, always managing to keep one leg from going into the post-chaise. Then, when all seemed lost for him, he saw another gang of navvies making their way towards him.

'Rescue!' he shouted, 'Come on! Come on!'

Side by side, with three pistols between them, Henry and George Schofield tried to hold the swelled mob, now numbering fifty or so, at bay.

'Stay back!' Schofield shouted, 'or we'll shoot!'

One of the navvies at the front said, 'You've only got three bullets and there's over fifty of us. Fire them and you're dead men.'

'That may be so my friend,' said Henry 'but I can assure you, that the first bullet we discharge will go right through the middle of your forehead. Now ask yourself this question. Is Dick Poacher worth dying for?'

The next few seconds, in which the man made his decison, seemed like an eternity to Henry, but he and his partner remained firm. To their relief, the navvy stopped moving toward them and his hesitation held the others back.

From behind them the magistrate called out,
'Come on, we've got him inside! Run for it!

Henry and George Schofield needed no further encouragement. They turned and ran towards the still stationary post-chaise. They were immediately chased by the gang of navvies, screaming for their blood.

Henry managed to pull himself up on the splinter-bar of the vehicle, whilst Schofield climbed up on the roof, where the magistrate was standing. Without thinking of the consequences, the excitable official shouted to the driver.

'Go on, man!'

The effect of the post-chaise pulling away so dramatically nearly had a fatal result. The magistrate and Schofield had nothing to hang on to and were nearly pitched, head long, into the marauding navvies, who were still in hot pursuit and throwing large flint stones. Both were saved from certain death by the quick wits and strong arms of the Tring brothers.

The post-chaise horses galloped away and soon

outstripped the angry mob. As they sped off towards Rugby, George Schofield called out to his friend, still mounted on the splinter-bar,

'How did you know the man wouldn't have called you're bluff?'

'I didn't,' said Henry.

• • • • •

A few weeks later Dick Poacher was tried at the county assizes and found guilty. Normally, he would have received the death penalty, as did his three accomplices the previous year, but Henry spoke up on the prisoner's behalf and he was sentenced to transportation for life. As he left the courtroom, Dick thanked Henry and apologised for biting and kicking him during his arrest.

Joe Bealey was happy too; he received his hundred pounds reward and no doubt soon exchanged it for several hundred tots of rum.

'We must be mad,' George Schofield said to Henry after the trial.

'Why's that, George?'

'To do this job. Everyone, from the Tring brothers to good old Joe has made money from this case. Even Dick Poacher escaped the hangman's noose, thanks to you. And what have we got out of it? Nothing! In fact, even with our expenses we're actually out of pocket! And yet we risked our lives to make the arrest. Why do we do it, Henry?'

Henry put his hand on his friend's shoulder. 'It's simple, George. We do it because we care. Come on, I'll buy you a drink.' He put his hand into his pocket. 'That's if you've got any money!'

CHAPTER SIX

'Mr Goddard, Sir,' said His Majesty William IV, 'you have done me and your country a very great service. Please accept this letter of commendation which I have personally signed.'

'Your Majesty does me a great honour,' said Henry.

The King's Private Secretary rolled his eyes to indicate that the audience was now over. Henry bowed and walked backwards until he reached the door.

He had first been summoned to the castle at Windsor over a year ago, in the summer of 1836. He had been assigned to follow the movements of the notorious Duke of Brunswick, a nephew of the King who, because of his outrageous behaviour, had made himself very unpopular with his own people in the German Duchy and with the British Press.

For the previous fourteen months, whenever it was reported that the Duke had entered England, Henry had to drop any case he was investigating and immediately locate the unpopular Duke and follow him.

The Duke often held clandestine meetings with known, 'agent provocateurs' and the British Government feared that he was plotting an assassination attempt on his uncle, the King.

When Henry returned home that evening and showed the letter from the King to Rose, she beamed with delight.

'Oh, Henry, I'm so proud of you.' She kissed her

husband on the cheek. 'I can't wait to show young William in the morning.'

'My love, he's only six years old,' said Henry. 'He won't understand the importance of the letter.'

Rose Goddard smiled. 'He will one day, and so will the rest of the children. You must pop round and show it to Sam Plank. He'll be ever so pleased for you and it will cheer him up. His wife says he's been murder to live with since he retired. When do you think you'll be summoned to see the King again?'

'Probably never,' said Henry.

'Why do you say that? He is obviously very happy with your work. Surely he won't ask for another Runner.'
    'From what I saw tonight,' said Henry, slipping into his fireside slippers, 'King William IV is dying.'

· · · · ·

Henry's fears for the health of his King were soon confirmed. On June 20th, 1837, William IV died. He had not been as unpopular as his brother, George IV, but his seven year reign did little to change public opinion about the monarchy. As he left no children to succeed him, the throne passed to his eighteen year old niece, a small, shy girl. She was crowned Queen Victoria in Westminster Abbey. Many in the country believed, including some Members of Parliament, that she would be the last monarch to sit upon the English throne.

Ordinary people, those who had never had any say in the running of the country and who lived hard, poor lives, in appalling squalor, sensed a new age coming. They realised the rich factory owners, especially in the north of the country, needed their labour. Some, whom the government called agitators, were determined that working people would have a share in the wealth which they were creating. They started to organise mass rallies to publicise their demands. They said that if the government did not listen to them, there would be a violent revolution.

• • • • •

Rumours about the abolition of all the Runner stations, including Bow Street, now began to circulate widely. On his retirement, Sam Plank had said to Henry that their days were numbered.

'The Iron Duke tried his best for us,' Sam said,'but now he is no longer Prime Minister, he has very little influence on the government, especially Sir Robert Peel. The world is changing, Henry, too quickly for my liking. The old order of things is beginning to break down. Everyone is shouting 'Reform!', 'Reform!'. People show no respect anymore. They openly ridicule the monarchy and they march in the streets demanding the country becomes a republic, and that working class men should get the vote. Where it will all end, I just don't know.'

'But some of the reforms that have happened recently, have been necessary Sam. The abolition of slavery in the Colonies and the improvement of working conditions for children in the factories and down the mines, are reforms that any decent Christian would welcome. And if the Runners are abolished, then I'm sure many will be recruited into Sir Robert's police force.'

'I suppose that's some consolation,' said Sam. 'We can teach them the true art of detective work.'

Although the rumours about the abolition of the Runners were disturbing, Henry tried to put them to the back of his mind. He had a job to do and he would continue to do it to the best of his ability until the end. Sometimes his dedication got him into hot water.

'What have you done, Goddard?' exclaimed Sir Fredrick Roe. 'How could you of all people be so stupid as to make an arrest without a warrant being issued.'

'But it had been issued, Sir,' replied Henry.

'Yes, but you didn't have it on you at the time!'

'But George Ruthven, took the said warrant with him when he was transferred to another case on the Continent. I did show the Count de Reiteroffer an old warrant, Sir. This seemed to satisfy him.

'Well, it didn't satisfy the sitting magistate. This Count de what's-his-name was released, after spending a week in jail! You're lucky he's not suing you Goddard.'

'As you say, Sir, the Count has very kindly refrained from taking legal proceedings out against me. Instead, he has promised to shoot me down dead if I ever try to arrest him again.'

'Well, dash it all, Goddard, one can hardly blame him, can one?'

• • • • •

Henry soon had the opportunity to put Count de Reiteroffer's threat to the test. A new warrant was issued for the Count's arrest for attempted blackmail of the Marquis of Downshire. He had been in the Marquis's service for some years and had travelled all over Europe and a great part of Africa with him. To his regret, it seemed that the Marquis took the Count into his complete confidence.

The Count's threat to shoot Henry did not deter him from his duty, although he did immediately make a will, leaving all his worldly goods to his wife and children.

The Count, however, could not be found. Henry made exhaustive enquiries over a period of several months, but it seemed as though the ground had just swallowed him up. The Marquis was convinced that the blackmailer had gone to Italy to escape arrest.

Then, one Saturday night, out of the blue, a man approached Henry as he was leaving Bow Street. He said, 'If you go to number 9 Arabella Road, Pimlico, you will find Reiteroffer,' he said. 'His room is at the back of the first floor. Go after 8 o'clock. But take care, he possesses a stiletto dagger and a pocket pistol and you know he will use them if he gets the opportunity.'

Before Henry could thank the informer, he had disappeared across the road between the cabs and the omnibuses.

Excited, Henry went back inside the Bow Street station to seek assistance. He found that all the Runners were out on duty and so he enlisted the help of Mr Tyrol, the station's jailer. The two immediately took a Hackney cab to the corner of Arabella Road. On locating the house, Henry went around the back and saw a light on the first floor.

'It seems he's in,' Henry said to Tyrol. 'I think the best thing to do is go in at the front door, climb the stairs and then give a really loud knock on Reiteroffer's door. If he opens it, then the two of us will rush into the room. But keep your wits about you; he may well have the pistol or stiletto in his hand.'

The two men gained entry to the house and quietly climbed the stairs until they came to Reiteroffer's room. Henry then knocked loudly three times on the door. After a pause of about thirty seconds, the door began to open very slowly. Through the gap, Henry saw a hand holding a pistol.

'Now, Tyrol!' he cried. The two of them rushed at the door, using their shoulders. They burst into the room. All three men were sent sprawling across the floor. Reiteroffer, his face covered with shaving cream, had the pistol knocked out of his hand. He grabbed hold of his open razor from his dressing table and held it menacingly out in front of him.

Tyrol picked up the Count's own pistol from the floor and pointed it at him. Henry pulled a document from out of his inside pocket.

'Count Reiteroffer, I have here a warrant for your arrest on a charge of extortion and blackmail. Please, come along quietly.'

The Count let the razor fall to the ground. He washed the lather from his face and then slowly dressed himself. He suddenly tumbled down onto a chair and complained of being unwell. 'I need a brandy,' he said.

'If you come quietly with us now,' said Henry, 'we will take you to the White Horse near by and give you a draught there.'

The Count agreed. He rose wearily from his chair and walked down the stairs, between his two captors, and into the waiting cab, which took them to the White Horse. Here, as promised, the Count was given a tumbler of cold brandy and water. He was then taken to the Grapes public house in Bow Street. It was not

unusual for the Runners to use this inn to keep prisoners, when their own cells were full. The room where the Count was to be kept had barred-iron windows and a very strong door; it would serve as an ideal cell until the prisoner could be brought before the judge on Monday morning.

Over the next thirty six hours Henry and Tyrol took turns to sit with the Count. On Monday morning, Henry went to collect his prisoner, but was shocked to see the Count's condition. The huge man was sitting in a chair in his shirt sleeves, his elbows on the table, resting his head on his hands. He looked a deathly blue all over.

'How long have you been like this?' asked Henry.

'Since about four o'clock this morning.'

Henry gave the Count some brandy and bathed his temples with vinegar. Then after a strong cup of coffee, he seemed to revive and declared himself ready to go before the judge. However, as they drove to the court, the Count fell into a state of half consciousness, so that he had to be almost carried into the procedings.

Henry was uncertain whether the Count was feigning illness. On previous occasions, he had avoided court appearances claiming, one time, that he had been wounded in a duel and another that he was sick with cholera.

Throughout the ten minute hearing, the Count sat, apparently unaware of what was going on around him. The judge ordered that he be remanded at the New Prison, Clerkwell, where he was immediately taken by Hackney coach.

Four days later, Henry was sitting at the breakfast table

with his wife and family, when there was a knock at the front door. On opening to the door he was given a written message from a young lad, who did not wait for a reply.

'What is it?' Rose Goddard asked her husband. 'You've gone all white.'

'It's the Count; he's dead. I've been summoned by the Governor of the prison.'

'But why, dear? Surely they're not blaming you for the man's death. From what you've told me, you treated him very decently.'

• • • • •

'I can assure you, Goddard,' said the Governor,'there will be a full inquiry as to the treatment of the deceased whilst in your care.'

'I welcome such a thorough inquiry Sir,' said Henry. 'I have nothing to fear from it.'

'We shall see, my man, we shall see.'

The following morning, Henry was summoned before the Coroner and asked to give his evidence. When he finished the Coroner asked,

'Don't you think the deceased looked like King Henry VIII?'

'I don't know, Sir,' replied Henry,' I never personally knew him.'

For moment he thought his flippant answer might get him into trouble, but after a few seconds pause, the Coroner began to laugh, as did the rest of the court.

'Very good, young man. Very good.'

Tyrol and the Governor of the New Prison were also called upon to give their evidence, after which the Coroner and the jury retired to consider their verdict.

Within the hour a verdict had been reached.

'It is the verdict of this court,' said the Coroner, 'that the man known as Count Reiteroffer, died of apoplexy due to an accidental overdose of opium. We find that there is no evidence to suggest maltreatment by the arresting officer. On the contrary, we would like to thank him for his efforts in the apprehension of the said Count and for the comforts he bestowed upon him. It shows, as ever, the value and importance to the community of the Bow Street Runners; long may they continue to serve their Queen and country.'

EPILOGUE

On Saturday, August 25th, 1839, the Bow Street Runners were dissolved. For ten years they had co-existed with Sir Robert Peel's new police force. The relationship between the two had not been a good one and it really was only a matter of time before one of them had to go. Many of the old Runners, not only those from Bow Street, joined the 'Peeler's' or 'Bobbies' as they became known. In June 1842, the C.I.D. was formed, taking over the detective work that had previously been done by the Bow Street Runners.

Henry did not join the London police. He became the first Chief Constable of Northamptonshire in 1840, on a salary of £250 per year. He resigned, owing to an injury he had received whilst on active duty in 1849, and received an annual pension of £150. It was not the end, however, of Henry Goddard 'the detective. He became a private detective and continued to chase criminals all over the world, into his old age. He also became chief doorkeeper at the Houses of Parliament and only retired from this post months before his death at the ripe old age of 83.

THE MUSEUM OF LONDON (071 600 3699)
18th and 19th Century Galleries: truncheons, other contemporary police equipment, history of law and order, graphic about development of London Police Service.

CITY OF LONDON POLICE (071 601 2705)
The City of London Police (37 Wood Street, London EC2) will be opening a small museum in early 1993. Displays will include leg irons, early uniforms, lamps, insignias, truncheons, etc.

YORK CASTLE MUSEUM (0904 653611)
A lot of 18th and 19th Century police related material. Also a reconstructed 19th Century street which includes a police station and a padded cell.

THE POLICE AND PRISON MUSEUM, RIPON (0765 609 799)
The museum is housed in what was once the Ripon Police Station and, before that, the local prison. History of crime and punishment (first floor) and development of the Police Force (ground floor) including an in-depth history of Victorian policing. Also an extensive collection of police equipment, including truncheons, handcuffs, uniforms, etc.

ABBEY HOUSE MUSEUM, KIRKSTALL, LEEDS (0532 755 821)
Truncheons, rattles and other 19th Century police equipment. Uniforms shown on request.

Several County Constabularies (Thames Valley, Greater Manchester and South Wales for example) also have their own small police museums. Visits by appointment.